Strategies To Build Successful Web Agency

GANESH GARAD

CONTENT

Introduction

Introduction

Hi, my name is Ganesh Garad, and in this book I'm going to give you tips about running a successful web design business, because I'll let you into a secret, knowing HTML and CSS is not enough to make you a successful web designer. You need to have those business skills, too.

What gives me the right to tell you that?

Well I guess it depends on your definition of what success is. On the surface the agency I run is nothing special. It's not really exceptional in the work that it puts out. It does normal work that anybody else does. We don't work for particularly big names like Coca-Cola or Nike, and we don't win lots of awards—mainly because we don't put ourselves in for them, but I think we are successful. My definition of success may be slightly different to a lot of people. For example, I don't believe success is the fact that we've been running for 12 years. It's not that we turn over a million and a half dollars each year, or that we have employees that range between about 13 people and 20. The numbers of members of staff don't really matter or even the fact that I take home a very healthy salary. It's that we have come to a point where we can now pick and choose the work we do. Work comes to us, rather than us having to chase it, and, most importantly, we've built a lifestyle business.

As the old adage says, "Don't live to work, but work to live." I will share with you the key things that have enabled me to achieve exactly that. I've broken down this book into six sections.

First of all there's marketing and promotion. How do you market and promote your business? Also, there's sales and pitching. When the leads come in how do you convert them? There's client services, how to keep those clients happy and then there's growing your business, but, most importantly, there are lessons about building a lifestyle business and actually getting work done in less time.

Marketing
And
Promotion

What Doesn't Work?

So let's look at the issue of marketing and promotion. I want to start by doing something slightly strange. I want to look at what doesn't work, because I think there are a lot of misconceptions and preconceptions surrounding how to market your work. Let's look at some things that don't work well.

In my experience cold calling, advertising, bidding sites, and networking events don't work very well. Now you might be thinking, "Well they work for me," and I'm not saying they never work. I'm just saying that I don't think they're the most effective way of working. So why don't these things work? Let's apply some of the principles of user centric design by putting ourselves in the place of our potential prospect our potential client.

First of all let's look at cold calling. The problem with cold calling by picking up the phone and just ringing someone you want to work with is that you have to call them at exactly the right time. They have to have a project that they want to work on there and then in order for your call to actually be useful. Now think about it for a minute. What are the chances of that actually happening, because if you're not calling them at exactly the right time all you're going to do is just annoy them, and they're certainly not going to want to work with you in the future if that's the case.

Then there's advertising, isn't there? The problem here is that there's just too much choice. There are too many people out there clamoring for attention, going, "Look at me! Look at me! Hire me!" The trouble is that you'll find that advertising gets really expensive, and you're just going to be one voice amongst a million clamoring for attention, and the problem is as well from a user centric point of view is that for most clients buying a website paying for a web design agency to come in and build them a web site is an important purchase and it's too important a purchase just to kind of go along to Google and click on the first ad. It's something that needs some kind of recommendation behind it.

Then there are those bidding sites, aren't there? You've seen them. You go along to something like Upwork and you enter in your details and you ask web designers to pitch, but my problem with those is it's all about price. They're the only things that define whether or not you win the work, so it all becomes a race to the button, and your profit margins will just evaporate into the air.

Finally, there are those networking events. My problem with networking events a lot of people really like them and enjoy them, and they are great fun. It's great to meet other people working in different industries and sectors, but my problem with them is that everybody is selling and nobody is buying. You'll go along to these events hoping that someone will buy your service, but if everyone

is selling then how are you going to win any
business through it?

So the big one is about hiring a salesperson.
Should you hire a salesperson to do all of this stuff
for you? Well that's a tricky question, and I have to
say. I don't think hiring a salesperson is the answer.
After all, how do you motivate them? Do you put
them on commission? but commission on what? Is
that commission on sales or commission on the
profit that you make on the project? If it's sales,
then they're just going to promise the earth, aren't
they? "Oh yes, we can do all of these really
complicated technical things on your website for 50
pence" because they want to win the project so that
they get their commission on that project. They
don't care that you're not going to make profit on it.
If however you provide them with commission
based on profit margins, well that's a bit unfair on
them, because your profit is so dependent on things
outside of their control. It's not their fault if the
client is badly managed. It's not their fault if you
get stuck on a particular technical problem. So it's
very hard to motivate an external salesperson.
So what is our conclusion from all of this? Well,
basically, traditional sales and marketing
approaches just don't work when it comes to
promoting your web design business.

Specialization

So here's the secret to successfully marketing a web design agency. You ready for this? Specialize. Now at first glance this may appear counterintuitive, because effectively what you're doing is you're narrowing the number of people that you can potentially get business from. By specializing you're saying, "I'm not doing this," or "I'm not doing that." That's a weird thing to do, isn't it? It will make you feel very strange, but there is a reason for it. At the end of the day, when it comes to marketing and sales you've got finite resources, and so you need to focus those resources where best they're used. Better to be regularly heard about by a small audience than heard about once in a blue moon by a bigger audience.

So, how do you specialize? Well, there are different options available to you. First of all, you can specialize in what you deliver, So you could go, "I only work on Ecommerce web sites," or "I only do WordPress websites." You get the idea. The second option is to specialize in the local area where you are, so you might be the best web designer in Pune, for example, or you can specialize across a market. For example, you could be a specialist in the charity sector, or a specialist at building school websites, or a specialist at doing hotel websites. It really doesn't matter.

Now once you've specialized, you can start focusing your marketing at a specific audience. You could focus right down at only talking to people that want an Ecommerce site, or only people within your local geographical area, or only people that want a charity website, a school website, a hotel website, whatever your specialty is, and the great thing is not only are these people now easier to reach because you're more focused, but you will gain a reputation as being the go to guy in that particular area. When compared to other web design agencies you're going to look so much more appealing because you're going to look like the expert.That is the wonder of specialization that it sets you apart from the crowd and makes you different.

Finding Your Target Audience

Okay, so you've made your decision to specialize. You've got to find that target audience, and that's not easy. You need to decide on who you're going to specialize with. Now a good place to start is by looking at your existing clients. That will give you an idea of whether there are particular groups of people that you've already got some experience with. What we did at my company is we realized that we'd done a real estate website, and we thought that might be an interesting sector to specialize in. We had a really good working relationship with the client, and so we went to talk to them, and I'd recommend that you do the same.

Go and find yourself a friendly client, sit down with them, and ask them about how they learn about their sector. Are there mailing lists that they're on that are dedicated to their sector? Are there forums that they read about their sector? Are there conferences that they attend? or meet ups? or is there a trade publication? You find a group that has some form of community around it. So with that higher education example I gave, there was very much a community of people that talked to each other through mailing lists, and forums, and all of those other kinds of things.

Once you have identified an audience like that a community that you can reach out to then things gets really interesting. So how do you go about reaching this audience? Well a good starting point is to participate in the community surrounding that audience. Mailing lists and forums are great. Join in the conversation, but remember, don't get too spammy. Don't push your services, but just give advice. Another thing that you can do is offer to write for trade publications or blogs because they're usually desperate for content and if you're willing to put in the time they'll probably publish it. Another option is to attend or speak at conferences. Going along to conferences is a great way of networking and building relationships with the community you're targeting, and if you can speak at them, all the better, although, admittedly, not everybody is a natural speaker. Finally, you can write for your audience as well. You can start putting out blog posts that use the right keywords that engage that audience and draw them in.

Ultimately, there is one aim here, which is to provide content and real value to your audience, not to spam them, not to market them in the traditional sense, but to provide them something tangible, and that is what we're going to cover in the next sections.

Providing Value

So you get the idea. The idea here is to provide real value to your target audience, and by providing them with value you're going to get them to pay attention to you. The key is to show your audience that you're knowledgeable about what you do and that you produce great work. That's the great thing about providing value is you're also showing how brilliant you are. The way to do this is to freely share your expertise. So how do you share your expertise? What's the key here? Well it's about finding the right medium for you. Everybody is different and you need to find what suits you. Some people are naturally good writers and so blogging is the obvious medium for you. Others, like myself, can do programming continuously hours and hours and so technical forums works well for me. You might want to run some kind of public Q and A, where you allow people within your target audience to pose questions to you and then you answer them in some way. Another option would be to offer a free consulting clinic where people can come to you with their questions about web design and you're there to answer them for them. Other options are giveaways. If you're not a natural writer or a natural speaker then maybe you're great at producing fonts that you want to give away. A designer friend of mine gives away WordPress templates, and that works great for him. If you're a developer you might be able to give away code snippets or plugins. There are so many options available to you. Webinars are another thing that I find an incredibly good way of engaging with your target audience.

The key with whatever approach you use is that you have to be continual. You have to keep doing it. Your target audience needs to continually and constantly see your name cropping up so that when they do have a project they're going to think of you, because they're constantly hearing about you. The other thing is you need to be regular. You need to keep constantly coming up with content on a timeline. The problem is that we often get really busy with work, so we stop blogging, or podcasting, or doing anything else, and then we hit a trough where basically the work dries up because we haven't been marketing it. We need to keep going.

We need our users the people we're trying to reach our target audience to expect our content and be waiting to hear from us. That's where we need to get when it comes to marketing.

Using Social Media

So you can't talk about marketing and promotion without mentioning social media. It would just be wrong to these days with Twitter and Facebook and all the rest of it. Social networks and communities are great way of building up your contacts within the target audience you is trying to reach. But as I implied earlier, it's really easy to annoy people. You got to be so careful that you don't spam people or harass people or just get under their skin. You need to be participating in these communities but it's always important to remember some basic principles when participating in communities online.

First of all, converse with people, don't broadcast them. Social networks are supposed to be about conversation, but so often when people are using them with marketing in mind, they just use them as a loud hailer to shout at people and that's not at all the right approach. Secondly, be personal. All right. Talk about yourself. It's a really interesting thing when it comes to sales and marketing that people buy from people. All right. They don't buy from other companies. They are attracted to people. Of all things that are equal, people are more likely to buy from you if they like you as a person. If they feel that they know you in some ways. So be personal when participating in communities. Also, as I said in the last section, make sure you're contributing value, answer people's questions, point them in the useful articles, join in with the community, be a member of the community rather than just marketing, act the community.

Also, if you get it wrong, you will get it wrong. You'll put you're foot in it at some point. When you do admit your mistakes, it really takes to win out of people's selves. If you've gotten in and you've accidentally been more salesy than you should have and people have gotten annoyed at you over it. If you go, yeah, hands up. You are entirely right. That was totally over the top. I do apologize. They got nowhere to go. So you can cover up a whole load of mistakes if you're just willing to admit it. Also, please, please, don't spam. Don't post so regularly. You get annoying. Whether it be a forum or on Twitter or Facebook or whatever else, you really can annoy people if you are just posting so much content.

One thing that people really do like when you're participating in social media, is when you share links, when you share content that you think your target audience might be interested in. And I'm not just talking about your content here, I'm talking about other people's content as well. It feels a bit weird sometimes when you post a link from one of your competitors but you actually really build up some respect amongst people and they think that you're not there just to sell at them because you're even willing to mention your competitors from time to time. And finally, ask questions. Questions are a great way of engaging a community. In the previous section, I mentioned about how we engage with the higher education community and one of the first things I did was ask questions. I showed an interest in the sector. I wanted to learn about it. And that was a great way to meet new people and engage with them online. So, if you want to promote your own stuff, there are all times and places where you can do that. Of course, there's no point of participating in a community if sooner or later you can't mention your own stuff. Yes, you can occasionally mention links to your own content but you could also use things like profiles and signatures to do it. People will go and look at your profile if they what if they're interested in your services, if they want to know a little bit more about you. So make sure that you make good use of your Twitter and your Facebook profiles.

If you're participating in forums, a lot of them allow you to insert signature at the bottom, and it is perfectly acceptable to mention your own site on there. If you're going to do anything more than that, however, make sure you ask permission of the community leader. So when I joined that real estate community I mentioned, the first thing I did was go and write to the community leader and I asked his permission to join in, to make sure he was okay with this evil corporate person joining his real estate community. And actually that worked really well. He allowed me to join but he made me promise that I wouldn't contribute to the community, that I would just listen and learn. So that's what I did and I took part in that community in a completely passive role for a long time until a question came up that I felt I could answer. And then I went back to the community leader and I asked that community leader's permission to answer the question and he said Sure, just don't sell your stuff. So I answered the question and little later, there was another question. So I repeated the process and I repeated it again and again and eventually, the community leader said, no, just post what you want, just don't be too salesy. So earned trust there and that's what it's all about when you're thinking about social media. It's to build up trust, build up credibility in the audience you are trying to reach to the point where they'll eventually accept you as their own.

Sales

And

Pitching

Pricing

So now we come to the subject of sales and pricing and all of that kind of nastiness. I don't know whether it's a Indian thing, we hate talking about pricing. It's embarrassing talking about money but we need to do it. It's a part of the job and we will need to face it. The first thing you need to work out is how you're going to go about charging your clients. Are you going to be fixed price or are you going to go time and materials? Now let's face it we do love to be time and materials. Didn't we?

It is much easier to manage and you get a much, well, you get paid for the work you do basically. But, a lot of clients are going to be nervous about time and materials. For them, there are no limits. The project could cost millions for all they know. And it requires a lot of trust before you get to that point. Time and materials does work but it works better with regular clients that you built good working relationship with and it's great for smaller pieces of work. Time and materials should always be associated with a rough estimate just to give the clients some sense of security, some sense that they know how big this project is going to be. If you do go down the time and material route, make sure you won the client well before you reached that estimate that you've given them. If you think it's going to pass the estimate, if you got any doubts at all, make sure you talk to the client. They really don't like surprises. But in most cases, fixed price is the way to go especially when dealing with new clients. But that does mean you need to add contingency to cover those eventualities that you haven't considered and make sure you do add those in because it can come back and bite you if you don't. The other important thing to remember when it comes to using fixed price pricing is to make sure that you don't forget the add on project management time because that takes a lot more time than you think.

Another really important thing to talk about when it comes to pricing and I admit this is not easy that you need to talk to the client about budget. How much have they got to spend? This is a really important question and a lot of clients, they really like talking about money. They've got this feeling that if they say to you they've got Rs.30,00,000 to spend, then inevitably the project is going to cost Rs.30,00,000 even if there's actually only Rs.20,00,000 worth of work. There's a lack of trust there. But, you really need to know. Don't you? You need to know how much you've got to work with. I used an analogy. I talked about houses and I asked the client, how much does a house cost? And inevitably the client has to say--well, it depends. It depends on how many bedrooms there are, it depends and where the house is, it depends on the market at the time. There were so many factors involved in buying a house and how much

a house costs. The same is true with web design.
For website, it depends on the technology that
you're using, the functionality that's required, the
amount of time that's dedicated, design or usability
testing or whatever else. Basically, a website can
cost as much as you're willing to spend on it.

Now, a lot of clients will get it at that point.
When you explained it like that, they will
understand, but there are always some clients,
there are always those that refused, that will not
give you even a vague idea of what they're budget
is. In such cases, the thing to do is give them a
rough estimate, a range that their website is likely
to cost. If that scares them off because it cost too
much, then you're better off finding out then before
you go to the effort of pitching for the work
properly.

When you do produce your final pricing,
make sure you break that pricing down into
modular chunks. Think of it in terms of core
functionality that has to be on the website and
optional items. So make sure that every item of
functionality on the website is priced individually.
This means that if your budget goes beyond what
they are expecting, then they can go through and
remove items or they can say that item was nice to
have, but at that price, we can't afford it or we can't
justify it. Break your pricing down wherever
possible. Also, if there are ongoing costs, make sure
to clearly identify that from. Things like hosting the
main names or indeed anything else that's going to

reoccur overtime. Clients kind of expect those things to be in a proposal and if they're not, then they become suspicious and wonder why there are now ongoing costs. The damage is the relationship and the last thing clients just despise the last thing that they want as prices so avoid those at all costs. So what is the secret here when it comes to pricing? The secret is a simple one. It's all about honesty. It's being upfront and talking about subjects that maybe a lot of us would prefer not to talk about.

Writing a Proposal

Another thing you have to do is part of the sales process is write proposals. Not very easy thing to do especially if really you're a designer or a developer at heart. But it's really important is your opportunity to standout from the crowd, it's your opportunity to grab the perspective client's attention. The first thing to do before you even start writing a proposal, is talk to the client, pick up the phone and have a chat with him before putting pen to paper. It's a chance to ask questions and a chance to show your expertise and start a conversation. It's a chance to build a relationship. Just receiving a printed document through is one thing but having a conversation with the client is quite another. It changes the whole dynamic of the relationship and increases the chances of you winning the work a hundred fold because you show that you care about the project, you ask intelligent questions, and you come across as the expert. You build a relationship. Don't be afraid to challenge the client when you have those conversations as well. Clients actually want you to provide alternative approaches. They don't want to spoon feed you. They want you to be the expert. So it's perfectly okay to may be suggest the old alternative approach to things.

So, when it actually comes to writing the proposal, how detailed should that proposal be?

Well the answer as with all things is it depends. It
depends on the size of the project for a start. If it's a
massive project, then they can expect the fairly
detailed proposal. If on the other hand it's small
piece of work, then really an email probably is
enough. It doesn't just depend on the size of the
project, however, it also depends on the depth of
the brief that you've received. If you received an
invitation to tender or request a proposal, whatever
you want to call it and it's really detailed, then
probably your proposal should be very detailed as
well. If they've not included so much detail, then
fine. You don't respond with this much detail. It's
important to understand the aims of the proposal.
Why are you creating one? Well, first is to
demonstrate your expertise. It's about giving a
sense that you know what you're talking about and
a sense of what it would be like to work with you.
Ultimately, it's all about providing confidence. A
confidence to the client that you can deliver on
their project. So what goes into a proposal? Well,
there's so many things that could go into a proposal
but they don't only to go in there for single one.
Like I said, it depends but some other things would
include a summary of the tasks. You need to write
out what you're going to do for the client. Fairly
obvious. Isn't it really? But you also need to cover
your suitability. What makes you the right choice
for the client? You need to talk about time scales.
And don't be afraid to be honest here. You're better
off saying if you're going to go over that time set

scales rather making promises you can't keep. Clients are often very grateful for the honesty in the documentation. And if you are saying that it's going to take longer than your competitors, then they might begin to wonder what the competitors are up to but if you are going to go over on the time scale, you need to justify why that is, otherwise, they're not going to believe you.

Then there is pricing. Of course, I've already mentioned that. That needs to be in your proposal as well. You also need to cover things like project management. How often is the client going to hear from you? How is the relationship going to work? Is it going to be via email? Will there be meetings? What's going on there? You need some back testing. What devices are you going to test on? Set some kind of parameters there; otherwise, they're going to be wondering why their website isn't working in all sense.

Hosting, we need to talk about that as well. That's a really important thing. Are they going to be hosting it or are you going to be doing that. Who's going to be managing that process and what costs that are associated with that? Discuss technologies as well. That's a really important area because you don't want to suggest the technology that their hosting environment can't support.

Most proposals also should include references. That's a really important thing. So that the client can go and talk to your existing customers and find out whether you're really as good as you claim. Finally, try and say a little bit about the team that would be working on the project. Why those people are suitable? If it's you--Why you are a great web designer? What makes you different? If it's with other people, make sure you show exactly who's going to be working on the project. Most of all, make sure your proposal is well written and visually engaging. Put as much work into your proposals as you do into your website. It is massively important that these documents are really, really good. Get somebody else to check it as well because that makes a huge difference. Ultimately, a proposal is your page. It's how you're presenting yourself to the client. So it needs a lot of time and lot of intention.

Speculative Design

So one of the things you might be wondering about as you put your proposal together is whether you should do some design mockups to show the prospective client. In fact, you might have even been asked to provide them as part of the tendering process. So should you be doing this kind of speculative design work? Should you be putting all of the effort in up front, without knowing whether you're going to win the work or not? Well, my answer is a clear one. No, you shouldn't. Well, almost never, anyway. There may be occasional okay, if Coca-Cola came to me with a multi-million dollar project and asked me to do some speculative design work, then maybe I would be tempted. But generally speaking, it's just a bad idea. And not just because of the amount of work you have to put into it.

Ultimately, it costs the client money as well. What? you might wonder. They're not paying for it. So how does it cost the client any money? Well, think of it like this, okay? Let's say a client comes to you and asks for some speculative design work, and you do it for them, but you don't win the project. Then you get another client come to you. Also asks you for speculative design work, which you do, and then you win the project. So that's two pieces of speculative design work that you've done.

You've not been paid for those, so how are you going to recover the cost? Because you have to. Your business has to be profitable. The way that you recover the cost is you build it in to the project you've won. So the project that you've won the client has paid for their own speculative design work, but they've also paid for the speculative design work for the client you lost. So it's costing them a lot of money, because you won the project. But that's not the only reason. It's not just about cost here. There's lots of other reasons why you shouldn't be doing speculative design.

For start, design is a process. You don't go into a room and sprinkle fairy dust, and this magical website appears out of it that looks good, you say it's perfect. There's a lot of discussion and conversation and backwards and forwards with the client. How can you do that before you've actually won the work? Any design you produce isn't going to take into account that process. Also, design requires a good understanding of the business you're working with. There's a lot of business analysis that goes into it. What are their business objectives? Who are their users? All of that kind of stuff. Again, those kinds of conversations don't happen before they've signed on the dotted line. So again, any design you work to produce up front is not going to cover that kind of stuff. Design should be a collaborative process between you and your clients. And that collaboration just cannot happen before that relationship has been established, before there's a contract in place.

At the end of the day, speculative design work can be nothing more than showmanship. It's nothing more than showing off that you produce pretty graphics. But somebody can look at your portfolio to see that. It can never be a true representation of what the final website should be. And although explaining that to the client is difficult, in a lot of cases you will actually get respect for doing so. We've been in situations where we've actually won work because we said, very up front, that we won't do speculative design work. And we've explained why. The client has been so impressed at our explanations, that they've immediately been cynical about any other web design agency that does speculative design work for them. If the client decides that they want that, and if you refuse and you lose the client, then ultimately it's a great way of weeding out undesirable clients that are going to end up being very difficult when you actually do the final work.

Pitching

I've got an embarrassing secret to let you into I really enjoy pitching. I really enjoy going in to clients and winning work, but I recognize that I'm weird. Most of us don't enjoy it. Most of us find the pitching process really quite difficult and quite cringe making. So let me give you some advice that maybe will make it a little bit easier and increase your chances of success of winning work.

First of all, be enthusiastic. It's amazing how far enthusiasm will take you. Just show that you care about your subject that you care about their project. It will go so far if you just look like you care. I once had a client say to me I'm embarrassed to say this, but it's true "How can I not hire you, it would be like kicking a kitten." And I just love that. I love that my enthusiasm and passion for the subject came across so much that that's what it was compared to. Being enthusiastic will take you such a long way.

But enthusiasm by itself is not enough. You also need to demonstrate your listening. If you get so over excited that you're not paying attention, things don't go well—trust me, I know. The easiest way to show you're listening to be honest is just repeating back to people what they've actually been saying to you but using different words. It's not really that complicated. You should be doing this in your proposal in responding to your RFP, but you can do it in the pitch as well.

Make sure that your client knows that you understand their challenges. So instead of talking about yourself and how great you are all the time, just pay attention to their needs. Talk about them and what they're struggling with. That's far more important than overselling yourself. You can look desperate if you talk about how great you are too much. Be sure to watch your body language. Not just your body language but more importantly, theirs. Are they nodding? Are they agreeing with you? Are they taking notes? Do they look concerned? If you're not sure what's going on—if for example somebody is looking a bit unsure or concerned about something, ask them. Say, "Do you understand what I'm getting at?" Or, "Does that make sense to you—are you happy with that?" Make sure you allow lots of time for questions and answers but don't overstay your welcome. So often a presentation can go on too long. You feel that there's so much that you have to say that you keep talking and talking and talking, although admittedly that might just be me, and you outstay your welcome. Make sure you keep the presentation short, have lots of time for questions, and you'll be fine.

Most of all please, please don't get demoralized. You will lose projects, and oftentimes when you do lose them even after a great pitch, it's for no discernible reason and not because you're rubbish or you've done anything wrong. Pitching can be hard, but if you don't let yourself get demoralized and keep up those enthusiasm levels, you'll be fine. It will all be great.

Client

Services

Why Client service Matters?

So we now turn our attention to the subject of client services. This is a bit of a weird one, and you might be wondering why I've included it. But the trouble is, as web designers we like to think of ourselves as manufacturers don't we? We build websites, that's what we do. But actually we're also a service business. It's not enough for our clients to have a great website. They also need to have a good experience. If they don't have a good experience, they're not going to love their website. If they don't love their website, they're not going to invest in it. If they don't invest in it, it's going to turn into a bad website no matter how much work you've put into it.

One of the best questions I ever got asked by a client was, "What are you going to do to make this web project fun for us to work on?" What a wonderful question. What a surprising question. What would your answer be to a question like that? It certainly caught us off guard, but it's a really good question. Because it's so important that clients enjoy the experience of working with you. It's not just important for the website and ensuring that the website is maintained and looked after. It's also important for you and your business.

An unhappy client who has had a bad experience will criticize you. And this is a particular problem if you take that specializing approach to marketing I talked about earlier. If you're targeting one particular community and you do a bad job and a client is unhappy for whatever reason, they're going to criticize you within that community, and word will get round and you'll struggle to win more business. Also the other problem is if you've got an unhappy client they could be more difficult to manage, and that's going to cut into your profit margins.

A happy client on the other hand one who is having a great experience and is enjoying working with you will recommend you, and that is absolutely invaluable. They'll be a brilliant reference, won't they, when it comes to adding references to future proposals. If you can include them then you can be sure of a good reference. Also a happy client is going to be more patient with you when things go wrong, and let's face it things always go wrong no matter how good you are as a web designer. But most importantly, if your client is happy they will come back to you again and again and again. And repeat business is ultimately the life blood of your business. If clients don't keep coming back to you, you're going to be in serious problems because repeat business has such a low marketing cost. You don't need to do a lot of things to attract people's attention because they already know you. Also the cost of sales is a lot lower. You won't need to be jumping through anywhere near as many hoops to win repeat business as you will for the first time. Also if they keep coming back to you time and time again, those turn into real high-value clients that are great. They're also a lot less hassle they know how you work, they understand how the process goes, and so your profit margins are going to be low tier. But most importantly of all, repeat business means better websites. If they're coming back to you again and again continually investing in their website, it's going to lead to better websites. And that is after all, what we're all about.

Fostering Repeat Business

So hopefully I've convinced you the value of repeat business. Now, the next question obviously is, "How do you win it? How do you keep clients coming back for more?" But the obvious thing is to focus on quality which seems so obvious. But when you're working with a client on an ongoing basis, it's easy to let quality slip over time. You begin to take that client for granted. You really can't do that. That's when you'll lose them so make sure you focus on quality all the time. Another thing I find really useful for keeping clients coming back is to do a post project debrief. So when a project ends, make sure you sit down with the client and talk about the project, talk about what went well and what didn't go so well. But also, talk about the future and what's coming next. Get the client all the time looking forward. And often, this will happen naturally anyway.

We'll mentioned about scope tree in a future section but one way of dealing with scope tree is to write down those ideas and say let's do in the next phase. Well, here is a great example of that. This is where you cash in on that because you can then come back in your post project debrief and say- "Look, these are the ideas we had. Let's do them now!" Do regular reviews as well with customers. Sit down with them, you know, once a year. Or once every 6 months. Or once every 3 months.

Whenever it is right and review where there site is at. And make sure that you have suggestions about where it should go in the future. Essentially what you're doing is trying to maintain a conversation. You're keeping talking to them. Keep them informed about latest innovations. Now you might want to do that with a newsletter that goes out to all of your clients.

But if you do that, make sure you also talk to some clients personally as well. Newsletters are great but they are a bit impersonal and it's really important to make suggestions for people-specific sites. Finally, show them what you've done with other clients. If you've done something cool within a particular sector say if you're focusing on charities for example. You do one great thing for one charity site. Show another charity client that and suggest that they might want to do the same. One of the most important things when it comes to repeat business is to be going above and beyond in what you're delivering. If the client feels that you are giving them real value for service, then they will keep back coming to you. So you have to go above and beyond. So one of the things that we do is we are conservative in our estimates. So what we will do is estimate that a project is going to take longer than may be we think it really will. And then we come in on to that and that impresses clients. That gives them the feeling we're going above and beyond.

Being proactive too is another great way of going above and beyond. So saying to clients, "Hey, why don't we do this? This should be a great feature. This should be a great idea." Now, most of your clients doesn't always have the budget to pay for these additional ideas. But you know what? Occasionally, I do that extra work for free. Not all the time because we don't want the client to get used to you doing work for them for free. But every now and again it's worth it. It's worth it to make the website better. But it's also worth it in order to show the client that you're going that extra mile for them. But if you are going to do extra work for them for free make sure you tell them you're doing that because the client needs to know that you're going that extra mile.

Now, the problem with repeat business is that you can find you become very reliant on a single client and this can be dangerous to your business. You got to be careful that if you're just working with one client all the time and they make up such a big part of your business then if they go away you're stuffed. So be very careful when working with just one or two really big clients. And to be honest, you're going to need to sit down with them and discuss it openly. Talk about the fact that it's a problem for your business but it is also potentially a problem for them that they're so reliant on one supplier. You might want to consider actually in such situations outsourcing some of that work that you manage and you still have the relationship but using other people so that you can develop other clients alongside that main client. But that said, repeat business is the way to go. It will make such a difference and you really need to be working on it right now to ensure that your clients keep coming back for more.

Clear Communication

If you want to keep your clients happy, talk to them. That's such an important part of good customer services. Clear communication. And it really is something you need to pay attention to. I once saw a tweet from a very well-known and well-respected web designer whose name shall remain nameless who said, "What does my client want from me? For me to build them a website or for me to e-mail them?" The truth is, a client wants both and you need to suck that up. You need to communicate regularly with your clients and you still need to be building them their website as well. One of the most important aspects of communicating with a client is to be regular. Contact them every week irrespective of whether you've done anything. Even if your call is just to say, "Hey, just to let you know. I haven't been working on your project this week. I've been working on another project, but it's absolutely fine. I've got time scheduled in next week. This is part of the plan, and I'm still going to be delivering on time." They would prefer to hear from you even if you have nothing to say to them. Because otherwise, they're going to wonder, and you don't want clients wondering. If they start wondering, they start worrying. If they start worrying, then they start micromanaging. And that is not something any of us want.

Another important factor with communication is the medium through which you communicate. Let's be honest. We're all geeks. And as geeks, we love e-mail and we love IM and we love BaseCamp. In fact, we love any medium which doesn't require us to actually talk to people. And so the result of that is that client's get frustrated because they're not like us. Some of them do like to actually talk to you on the phone. So what you've got to do is use the medium that's most appropriate to them. If they like using BaseCamp, hell, use BaseCamp. If they like using e-mail, then yeah sure use e-mail. But if not, then you need to be using what they like and not what you like.

With communication, always tell the truth even if the client does not want to hear it. You're much better off limiting their expectations so that you can later surpass them than you are to essentially lie to the client. The trouble is we don't intentionally lie to them, right? Let's say there's a deadline that's coming up. And we're beginning to wonder whether or not we're going to meet that deadline. And we go, "It's okay. I'm going to make the time off. I'm going to work over the weekend and I'll get it done because I don't want to let this client down." And so we work weekends and we still sleep in and deadline's getting closer. And it's all getting full but no we're going to do it. We'll work. We'll work through the night to get it done in time. And then eventually, we fail. And we've lied to the client. We told them everything's going to be alright and it isn't. We've given them a nasty surprise and as I've said before, we don't want to surprise clients. They don't like that.

So, if you're worried about meeting a deadline. If you perceive that there might even possibly be a problem with the project, tell the client. You're better off telling them and lowering their expectations and then everything turning out all right and the client goes away happy than you are leaving them with a nasty surprise.

Meet with your clients often, will you? Take the time to go and meet with them. When failing that, use the phone. Make sure that you're engaging with them personally because it will really help the communication and the relationship between you and the client. That said, when you do meet them or if you do have phone calls with them, make sure you keep notes and records of what's been said too and repeat that back to the client. Having a written record is often very useful when things go wrong. So communication is vitally important and it should be considered a fundamental part of your job as a web designer.

Dealing with confrontation

So I'd like to tell you that if you've follow all of my guidance about client services every client project will be wonderful or we'll all live in this happy Utopian world and everything will be great. Unfortunately, I can't tell you that. It'll be a nightmare. There will be times when things go wrong. There will be times when you have problems, you fall out with the client, and aaah! What do you do? Dealing with confrontation is unfortunately an important skill that you will need sooner or later. I'm sorry about that but that's just the way things are.

My first piece of advice for this is keep calm. Just because the client is angry, don't allow yourself to go down that route as well. Just because they raise their voice, doesn't mean you should. It's much better to keep calm that it is to get angry. Acknowledge if you've done something wrong but also acknowledge that the situation has reached this point and apologize for that. Whether or not, you've messed up or whether the client has been unreasonable, it's still your responsibility to stop these kinds of problems and you should apologize if things have gotten this far. And, don't do that non apology thing. I'm sorry that you feel like that. That's not an apology. That's just a platitude. But you're sincere in your apologies. It does make huge difference and admitting your mistakes will take a lot of the wind out of themselves.

It's really important to identify the underlying problem here. Often what a client gets angry about isn't actually the root of the problem. They might be annoyed because the design is not what they wanted or that you've misunderstood their brief or whatever else but actually the underlying problem might be "I don't feel you've listened to me." So you need to work in identifying what that underlying problem is. Be sure that you get to the root of the problem before going any further. Also, another thing is like a dumb thing but ask the client what they want. If they're unhappy, you often get into this argument about what it is that they are unhappy about and you focus on the problem and not the solution. Instead of focusing on what's gone wrong, say to the client, "Okay, what can I do to fix this? What can I do make you happy?" and then do it. Fix the problem. Whatever it takes you got to go for it, you got to fix the problem. And then, because you've asked the client what they want you to do and then you've done it, then you can say, "Are you happy now?" and of course they have to be happy because you've done exactly what they've asked. It's not always possible but it's a general rule of fun but it's not bad.

Once you've fixed the problem, get feedback on them. Get them sit down and say, "Are you happy now? Is there anything else I can do?" Take stock as well. With the client, sit down with them and say, "Okay. Where are we at? Do we feel that things have been resolved properly?" and then demonstrate to the client that you're going to avoid a repetition of this situation. Learn from what's happened and correct the problems so that it's not going to happen again.

Now, most of the time this will sort things. Just occasionally, it doesn't. There are really things have gotten very badly wrong. Now, there are lots of options available to you here but the one that I tend to prefer and I tend to use is I essentially reboot the project. I will say to the client, "Okay. Look. This we've just gotten off the rails really badly here. Let's go back to basics. Let's start again and begin the project again." And often, although that screws your profit margins, it will fix the project. And, sometimes it's better to go back to the very beginning than it is to put plasters on the problems to try and cover up the issue.

Starting a fresh is often the best way to go. Failing all of that, walk away. Know when to walk away. The point comes with some clients where you just have to go--"Look, we're not the right fit for one another. It's not happening for whatever reason and it's time to go our separate ways." I think that should be a last resort but is there for you. Don't rush in to that option but know when to do it when it comes to it.

A

Lifestyle

Choice

Planning For The Future

So last few thoughts I want to leave you with before we move on from this area of creating new business is planning for the future and thinking about the future. The trouble is you can get so caught up with the day to day work of dealing with clients and all their problems and the challenges of keeping up-to-date with the latest web techniques that we don't spend enough time to think about the future of all businesses. We need to be really careful that we plan our businesses properly and we're always looking ahead to the next step.

So, is it really important to stay focus and not to over stretched yourselves that we can get so ambitious with our plans sometimes and start so many different things that we never follow through. So there is a balance to be struck here. With planning for the future, trying new stuff, but also not over stretching ourselves. The key here is to set aside regular time to think strategically about where we're going with our business. It's so hard to do but so incredibly important. So let's take a moment to consider how we go about setting aside that time and what we do with that time when we have it.

The first piece of advice I would provide is consider getting an outside perspective. At our company, we have a non executive director that is not involved in the day to day work of our web design agency at all. Instead, we get him in to provide a fresh perspective. This has a couple of benefits. First of all, it means that there are designated times when he is coming in that we have to stop day to day work and think strategically about the future direction of the company. The second benefit is he encourages us to think in ways that we've never thought before. Because he is outside of the business, he provides a perspective that we can never have if somebody that works day to day in the business. He provides that different perspective you need, and you need to find somebody that does view the world very differently to you. For example, the person that we have is our known executive director. He is used to working with companies that have an exit strategy, that build up and then they're sold off by the owners. So we are very different for him because we run a lifestyle business. But, he is constantly challenging us to maybe be more ambitious in our plans for the business. So having someone with a different perspective is hugely useful.

Another piece of advice when it comes to planning for the future is to stay flexible. It's so easy to get entrenched in ways of working. And see you always need to keep an eye out and ask yourself, Are the things that I've done in the past still relevant in the future? For example, it's so easy to get so deeply entrenched with the particular technology or particular way of working that when something new and radical comes along it's too much for us to cope with. Maintaining that flexibility is the secret to running a successful business long term.

You also need to be willing to take calculated risks. We've done so many things as a company where we've tried new areas where we branched out into different directions. Some of those have succeeded but I have to be honest, a lot of them have failed and you need to do it anyway. Don't let failure demoralize you. Make sure you've got good cash reserves behind you to support you when do make mistakes. And you'll be fine. Winston Churchill said the best quote that I love more than anything else and I apply it everyday when I think about growing my business. The quote was "Success is going from failure to failure with no loss of enthusiasm."

Work to Live, Never Live to Work

So let's move on and look at the crucial thing for me and the thing that we discussed right at the very beginning which is this idea of building a lifestyle business. A business that supports the life that we want to live. Work to live. Never live to work. There are basically two types of businesses. There are those with an exit strategy and there are those lifestyle businesses that are developed to facilitate the lifestyle that you want to live.
Now as you have gathered, I'm a huge fun of the second type of business and I think most web designers fall into this category. They like the idea of building a business that supports their lifestyle. People become their own boss for a couple of reasons. Firstly, they have this image that if they become their own boss and set up their own business, they'll have more time. They'll have more money and more freedom in what they do.

Unfortunately, the reality is not always that. I've got to say that a lot of the freelancers and web designers I know that who've gone and set up by themselves, they're undercharging from their work a lot of the time and they're also at the whims of clients. Essentially, all of those things that they wanted from setting up their own businesses, they failed to achieve. Now they tend to justify it to themselves by saying that things will get easier but I have to say to you, don't live for the future. Your business should facilitate your lifestyle today. And so don't set up the business where you're willing to sacrifice those ideas you had when you first set it up. You wanted more freedom. You wanted to work less hours. You wanted to be your own boss. Hang on to that. Ask yourself, what was your perfect job be like? And then keep focused on that vision. If your perfect job is working less, make sure you work less. If you're getting too busy, either hire another member of staff or don't take on as many projects. If your perfect job is to be your own boss, make sure you don't take on that project which you know has got a really difficult client who's going to turn into a pain in the neck. If something is going to take you further away from your vision, don't do it. Stay focused--Remember, you're in control of your business and not the other way around. It's easy for your business to turn into this monster that you have to constantly feed with work and it ends up dictating to you but that's not the way it should be.

Ultimately, a lifestyle business is about facilitating your lifestyle but remember this as well, it's not just about facilitating your lifestyle, it's also about facilitating the lifestyle of your employees too. If you've hired someone, that's not an excuse to dump all the rubbish on them because you don't want to turn into one of those bosses. You're trying to create a business that facilitates the lifestyle of everyone that works in it. Stay focused on their aim and I can promise you that you will enjoy your work so much more and you will enjoy working with your colleagues.

Your Attitude on Money

Another important aspect of running your own business and creating a lifestyle business is to tackle the issue of money and your attitude towards it. This is an important part of what we do. We don't talk openly enough about money. Now one of the biggest questions that all freelancers and web designers had to work for themselves ask me is how much should I charge? And to be honest, I can't answer that question for you. There's too many variables such as your location or your skills set, all the type of clients you work with. It's not something I can help you with but what I can tell you is that chances are you're probably charging too little. There are loads of things that we forget to consider when we set our charge out right . We have this notion in our heads that we'll be able to work everyday and charge out all of our time but it doesn't work like that. We're going to have loads of overheads that will also increase our costs. We've got sales and marketing time.

Today is a big chunk of your time that's not going to be chargeable. Then of course there's admin and project management and things like that. Occasionally , you might even want to take a holiday perish the thought, and you're not going to get paid when you do that. What if you get sick? You've got to cover those cost as well. And then, of course there are taxes that we will have to pay whether we like it or not. You also need to consider what you're going to take out of the business. Your rates dictate how much goes into the business but what about your salary. A lot of freelancers and other web designers don't set themselves a specific salary but instead take money out of the business as they feel that the business can support it but I will encourage you give yourself a set salary. It will make budgeting and planning a lot easier but more than that, I think It sets a stronger separation between company finances and personal finances. You can get yourselves into all kinds of trouble if you just dip into the business whenever you feel like it. So have a set salary and then stick to that.

Now, be fair about that salary and give yourself something reasonable otherwise what's the point of being a freelancer but try and be realistic as well. You need to be fair not just to yourself but also to your staff. And when it comes to staff, I would encourage you to reward early adopters. The first people that come and join you because that's quite a big risk for a lot of people to join a small company. So what we do is we tend to give them a good salary and we may also give them share options or things like that for the early joiners. But, you equally need to reward yourself because you're taking the risk as well as setting up your own business to make sure you give yourself a good salary as well as those first one or two employees.

The other thing I encourage you to consider is bonuses. Although having a set salary is a great idea, if your business is doing particularly well, there's nothing wrong with rewarding yourself for that success and having good bonuses is a way of doing that. Not only should you be giving yourself good bonuses but you should also be considering this for any members or staff you take home. Reward them when things go well, make sure they benefit as much as you do from the success of your business. Also, even when things aren't going so well, if someone has gone above and beyond and worked really, really hard, then reward them in some way even if it's a quite low level.

Finally and most importantly when it comes to money, don't starve your business of working capital. Yes, you want to pay yourself for good salary, yes, you want to give bonuses but make sure you always got a buffer behind you for those tough times. I would say if you can have as much as 6 months of salary behind you in the bank. That's not always feasible but it's something to work towards.

Investing in People

One of the most important things when running a lifestyle business is to invest in your people. Now when I say your people, I'm not just referring to your employees, I'm referring to you as well. It's just as important to invest in yourself as it is to people you take home. If you do have a team, socialize with that team. Build a team spirit. You need to be a group of people that come together and do fun stuff together. It shouldn't be all work all the time. Otherwise, you're going to drive each other mad before too long. If you're by yourself, I encourage you to get out and meet people. It can be a very lonely and isolating experience running your own business and it's so important to hang out with people that are in the same situation as you. So I encourage you to go and meet up, conferences all those kinds of things, any opportunity to hang out with other freelancers and web designers. You need to be interacting with other people that are working on the web and you certainly need to grab every opportunity that's available.

Another really important part is to invest in yourself through reading. Now you already know this. You see in here, reading this book right now. Of course you know that reading is important but you also need to make sure that all your other members of staff have the opportunity as well. I'm also sorry to break it to you that reading this book isn't enough by itself. There are other things you can do as well. You can attend conferences. That's great. What about watching some other training courses?

The most important thing is to set aside time to learn and experiment. For example, I know of many web designers that set aside a day or week for personal projects. An opportunity to try out new things and all the stuff that you're learning on courses like this. Training is important but so as time to recuperate. We push ourselves too hard as business owners. Keep working hours under control. I know a lot of you love your job, you love playing with the web, you love technology, you're a geek at heart but that doesn't mean it's healthy or good for you to be working long hours. You need to have generous holidays. You need to have interest beyond the web. Yes. There are things like real life too. Get out there. Do other stuff. Christmas for example. Consider closing down over Christmas. Nothing ever happens anyway. No work gets done between Christmas and New Year. So why bother working? Have a life beyond web design. It will improve the quality of your work and I'll tell you something else, they'll win you more business.

Controlling Growth

So if all goes well you're going to find yourself pretty busy pretty soon, and that's an exciting problem to have, but also controlling your growth is something you really need to pay attention to. As things go along, and you bring in new work, and you get a reputation, it's very easy to get into a situation where you start recruiting more and more people. It's probably a little premature for many of you to be thinking about this now, but just bear it in mind when you come to that day. Only recruit as a last resort. Staying small has a lot of benefits to it. Don't long after having a big company with lots of employees. Whey you stay small you've got less mouths to feed, and that means you got more control over your business and what work you do. You can pick and choose clients rather than having to take anything that comes through the door just to keep people busy. Also when you stay small, you have that ability to pick and choose, and that's such an important thing in terms of the quality of life and enjoying the work you do.

The last thing you want to be doing is working on projects you don't find particularly engaging. It's hard to do that mind. Turning away work feels so difficult, but you need to be strong. Turn away projects that don't fit you, don't fit the kind of stuff that you want to do, and set realistic deadlines. Don't agree to do projects that are going to mean you are so overstretched that you have to take on employees. If you find it hard to turn away work or have more work than you can handle, I suggest trying to raise your prices. That's a great way of reducing the amount of work you get coming in. What a weird problem to be talking about. The fact that you want to reduce the amount of work. But the time should come, and increasing your prices is a good way to do that. Obviously you do that sensibly and over a period of time. You don't suddenly whack them up, although I know of one web designer, a guy called Mahesh, who doubles his prices on Fridays just to see what will happen. I think that may be a little bit of an ambitious thing to try but give it a go. Try incrementally increasing your pricing over a period of time and see whether that controls the number of projects you get coming in.

Be careful of contracting out work. As I've already said, it has a lot of disadvantages to it. You really only need to do that as an absolute last resort. Also the bigger that you get as a company, the more personnel problems you're going to have to deal with. Sometimes you can feel like you're more of a manager than you are a web designer anymore. Know when you've got too big. You'll be able to sense it. You'll see your stress levels increasing, and if you reach that point you need to know that it's time to shrink. Remember you don't get rewards for having lots of employees. Having lots of employees does not make you a successful web design agency. It's about having an enjoyable job that you love to do, and if having too many employees creates a problem with that then maybe it's time to reduce them. But that doesn't mean that you have to fire people. I'm not a great fan of that. I hate making people redundant. You will find that people naturally move on over time and just allow that to happen. So control your growth. Be the size you want to be. Don't allow your company to take on a life of its own while you're just running to keep up.

Getting

Work

Done

Establishing the Right Working Practice

In this last section that we're going to look at, we're going to discuss the area of getting stuff done. All of this talk about growing your business is worth nothing unless, of course, you can get the work done. So the key here is to establish the right working practices. If you get that right, everything will go smoothly. If you're going to keep your hours under control because you're building a lifestyle business, and that's what you need to do you need to start working smarter, but not necessarily longer. Also, being your own boss means that you need a structure in order to stay motivated. If you don't have that structure in place, you're going to lose motivation quite quickly. There's also a need to keep clients happy. And they're going to be happy when they feel that you are in control. And that means you've got to be organized. You need a system in place. You need a method of dealing with what I think are the three major productivity killers: distractions, the client, being unorganized. And that is what we're going to look at in the rest of this section.

Dealing With Distraction

If you want to get stuff done, if you want to work less hours and earn more money, you need to deal with the distractions that surround you everyday. The starting point for that is being aware of what they are, and boy are there a lot of them in the world of a web designer. There is instant messaging, there's Twitter, Facebook, RSS, web browsing, email, phone calls. The whole environment can be distracting if it's not designed right. You need to take some active steps to remove those distractions. Otherwise you're going to find yourself working at midnight every night. Now if you're a night owl that might be perfectly fine, but you don't want to be working from 6 in the morning too. First thing you need to do is get rid of Twitter and Facebook. Don't have them constantly open. I know this is a stupid little thing, but it makes a huge difference to the amount of time you work. I'll let you in on a secret. Most days I only work about 6-½ hours. Reason? Closing Facebook and Twitter.

Well at least some of the time anyway. Keep your whatsapp activities to a minimum.Also, I'm talking about things like RSS, web browsing, all of those things that you do as a distraction from what you should actually be doing. One of the ways of doing that is to isolate those activities away from your work environment. So in other words, do your web browsing and your RSS feeds and your social networks and that kind of stuff—do it on your iPhone or your iPad, not on your work machine. Get them out of sight while you're trying to get stuff done. Another piece of advice when it comes to getting work done is never try and multitask. It just doesn't work. We don't, as human beings, have the capability to multitask. Yes we can switch very fast from one task to another, but that's not the same. Moving from task to task will ultimately slow you down. If you're somebody that struggles to concentrate for a long length of time like myself—I consider me to have the attention span of a small child—but the way I get round this problem is by working in sprints. There's something called the Pomodoro Technique which is really simple. You work for 25 minutes, you have a 5-minute rest, and then you work for another 25 minutes. So you have 25 minutes solid on one task before moving to another. So it means that you can get significant work done.

Talking of distractions, turn off those automatic notifications. I calculated, for example, that with the average email client like Outlook, on its default settings you will get interrupted 31,680 times per year by that little ping notification of a new email coming in. Now that is a huge amount of interruptions, and let's be honest, every time it pings we have to go and look even though 90% of the time it's just spam and doesn't matter anyway. So turn off those notifications. You don't need to spend your whole life in your email client. Only answer the phone or check email or even IM at set times within the day. That's why the sprints work quite well because you can have certain sprints at certain times of the day for making phone calls or answering email or using IM.

Now you might be getting a bit twitchy at this point. The thing is closing email, not answering the phone, and not having IM on is very alien to us as web designers. We're used to being connected all the time, and most of us can't comprehend a world where we're not constantly checking email. What if a client has an urgent inquiry? What if they need me to do something right now? I can understand that and that fear of being out of touch, but the reality is 90% of the communications that come in are not time-sensitive. So all of those interruptions disrupt you from the work you should be doing, but for those 10% of communications that are urgent, I'd encourage you to look at various tools out there that help you manage it. For example, there is a tool which basically allows you to identify certain emails that you know are urgent from a certain person or mentioning a certain keyword, and they will then forward those on as a notification to your phone. That way you don't need to have your email client open the whole time, and you will only be interrupted with the most vital of emails.

There are also virtual services that will answer the telephone for you. For example, in the

U.K. there is a service called moneypenny, but there are equal other services in various other countries that provide the same service. What you do is you forward your phone number onto this, and a real person will answer the phone, take a message, and will contact you if it's urgent. So there are ways where you can close down those distractions, where you can close down email and the things that interrupt you allowing you to get big chunks of work done without alienating clients and without getting all twitchy.

Client Related Challenges

So we've stumped on our distractions. But the next problem—the one area which is very hard to ignore is the client. We might be able to turn off our email some of the time, but that doesn't mean we completely remove clients from the equation. And clients do damage our productivity whether we like to think it or not. Or whether they like to think it is more to the question. Meetings, calls, emails all eat into our actual productive time of getting work done. Then there's scope creep, which screws with our scheduling and our profitability. We have this project all planned out wonderfully, but then suddenly the client wants something else that we hadn't planned. It's that whole unpredictable nature about clients where you don't really know how long it's going to take them to sign off a design or whether they're going to quibble over a particular aspect.

Now all of those things need addressing, and we need techniques for dealing with working with clients. Now we've already addressed the issues of telephone calls and emails and suggested there are some things you can do there, but there are other things too. Take for example meetings. Always schedule your meeting with a client even if they're nearby. Even if it's a client that you could easily pop in to see, don't just have ad hoc meetings. Make sure they're scheduled into your calendar so that they happen when you want them to happen, and they don't just suddenly interrupt you in the middle of something else. Another useful technique is to make use of video conferencing. This limits the amount of travel time to see clients. Now I said earlier that meeting face to face with clients is really important, and I stand by that. But not every conversation with a client needs to happen face to face, and a lot of the time you can use video conferencing to do that. Always, always set a time limit on a meeting with a client. Don't allow it be an open-ended meeting, and also don't feel that you always need to go with a default that a calendar is set up for. Most calendar apps will automatically set a meeting as being an hour long. And for a lot of meetings, that's too long. So what we tend to do when we have meetings with a client is we make it very clear that we need to stop by this time because we have other commitments that follow on from there. So arrange your meetings with that end time in mind. But also try and group the meetings together so that you're not constantly begin interrupted through the day. Have an afternoon or a day a week which is dedicated to meetings so that you're not constantly interrupting your time spent building the website. Always have an agenda going in for a meeting as well. So many meetings turn into these open-ended discussions that don't really go anywhere and drag on endlessly. Have an agenda and stick to it. And say up front that you have to be done by a certain time. There's also scope creep to consider as well.

First thing to do for dealing with scope creep and stopping a client getting carried away is to have a written specification. Outline exactly what it is you're supposed to be delivering, and insure that everyone is signed up with that specification. Then if something comes along that isn't in the specification, it's clear. And there's none of this, well, I thought it was going to be included. That happens so much and can throw out your projects. Be realistic and honest with your clients about ideas that they come up with. If an idea is easy to implement, feel free to implement it. But a lot of the time you want to push ideas back into a second phase. I recommend keeping an ideas list between yourself and the client that when they come up with new ideas, put it down on the ideas list. That's where these new things go. They don't get rolled into the project so making it longer and longer. Review the ideas list at the end of each project, and that can turn into the repeat business we talked about earlier. Finally there's unpredictability, those aspects of client behavior that are hard to predict and can really throw out a project. Communication is a key aspect of that. If you're communicating with them often, then these things are less likely to arise. Also avoid surprises.Show your client stuff often. A classic example of where this can go wrong is with design. Designers like to work in isolation. They like to go away and produce their beautiful designs and then present them to the client in this ta-da moment. The problem with that approach is the client is surprised with a completed design that may or may not be in line with their expectations. If you had shown them sketches and mood boards and wireframes and all of these other things along the way, then you would have identified problems earlier on rather than having this problem hit you after you've spent a lot of work and a lot of time working on a design. So show the client often what you're doing. Adding contingency as well to projects.

Make sure that there is ample time for these unpredictable things that clients tend to do from time to time. And when they do say something that surprises you, that sets the project off in a different direction, that is unpredictable, don't go in and just say, no, I'm not going to do that because that doesn't help with the client relationship. Instead explain the consequences. Point out to them that if did this, it would have a knock on effect on the project. Most importantly, make sure that the client understands that they might only be adding a day's work onto the project with something that they suggest, but that doesn't necessarily equate to just a days delay in the overall time of the project. The reality is you have other commitments with other clients. And this—your clients wouldn't like it if their project was pushed because of another client. So if you set a certain time to work with a certain client, you need to stick to that. So if the previous client overruns, then it's going to be a while before you can come back to that project. So there you go. Working with clients is never easy and does have an effect on your productivity. You're not going to get to sit endlessly coding without having to deal with clients. But working with clients is something that's manageable. If you set meetings that happen at a particular time, if you have a way of dealing with scope creep, and if you have methods of dealing with the clients unpredictability, then you will get a lot done, and the client doesn't need to dominate your day.

Getting Organized

So your final big productivity killer the final thing that you need to sort if you're going to run yourself a good lifestyle business so you can sit back and enjoy the world is you need to deal with being unorganized. Are you organized? Do you have a system? How do you organize yourself? There are probably four steps to successfully organizing yourself as a freelancer. Those are setting aside dedicated time to organizing things rather than just building websites. Sorting email is a big one. Get it out of your head, and then delegate it. Those are your four options, and we're going to cover each of those in this section.

So let's begin by dedicating a block of time to being organized. What I recommend is at the beginning and the end of everyday you sit down and review what you're doing. At the beginning of the day you review what you're going to be doing that day what you've got laid out for you. At the end of the day I recommend making sure you've covered everything through the day and then scheduling at least an idea of what you're going to doing the next day. It can, if you're feeling really busy, feel like a waste of time, but boy it's not. This is by far the most valuable thing you will do.

Another thing you might want to do is set aside a little bit of time each week to do a more comprehensive view of everything that's going on. Set aside blocks of time for emails and phone calls, as I suggested earlier. And ring fence large blocks of time for actual production, especially coding. The worst thing in the world is being interrupted while you're coding something. You lose your train of thought, and you can waste a lot of time trying to get back in the zone again. When it comes to designing, I would encourage you to allow time to think about your designs. Design is a funny thing. You can't sit down and just churn out a design. Often it needs to kind of go around in your head for a while, so make sure there's enough elapsed time just to think about your design before you actually crank open Photoshop.

I think another really important thing to do when it comes to running your own business is to work around your own natural body clock. We're all different—who says we should work 9 to 5 every day? If you are your own boss, you can work whatever hours you like, can't you? Some of us, like myself, are early morning birds. And so start early in the day and work into the evening a little bit. Whatever works best for you. Make sure that you're doing dedicated production work when you're at your most productive.

Another thing that you really must do is sort email. So many people's emails is just chaotic, but it's such an important tool in our business lives, and we do need to take control of it. If you're one of these people that have got thousands of emails sitting in your inbox, I recommend right now you declare email bankruptcy. You email out everybody in your inbox and say, "Look, I'm really sorry, but I'm starting again with my email. I'm going to file everything. If there is something that you need from me that I haven't responded to, please send me a new email." You need to get control of your inbox because ultimately your inbox and your email should be a place where tasks come in, you process them, and then they go out of your inbox. This is a thing called Inbox Zero. If you haven't heard about it, check it out because it will make such a difference in how efficient you are in managing email. Also with email, forget folders. I see so many people that get carried away with organizing their emails into hundreds of folders related to every client and project and all of the rest of it. Search is so powerful these days that you really don't need to be doing that. Make better use of filters and rules, and use something like Gmail. That can be an incredibly great way of getting rid of so much stuff that comes into your inbox that you don't need to be dealing with immediately. There are some great tools for using email these days. If you haven't checked out Mailbox for the iPhone, check that out. Great tool for using email as a task list basically. There are also services which allows you to bundle up all those newsletters and other things that you read and address them once a day rather than pinging every time something comes into your email client. Another little tip if you want to reduce the amount of email you receive is to send less. The less email you send out, the less you will get back. Reduce the number of emails, but also reduce the length of your emails. If you write short, snappy emails that get to the point, you'll find that over time people start replying in the same way, and you can save yourself a lot of energy and effort there. And then, as I've already said, only check email occasionally. To be honest, I'm at the point now where I check it first thing in the morning, lunchtime, and last thing at night. And that should be enough if you've got the right systems in place.

Another important aspect of being organized is to get all of those tasks that you have to do out of your head. Your memory is rubbish, it's not the place to hold all of this information. You will forget stuff, and you will annoy clients. You need something more concrete than holding it in your head. Basically our memories just don't work particularly well, and also we put stress on ourselves if we don't have a nice organized place to hold all the tasks. We try and hold it in our heads. We try and—but we end up going over and over and over it, and that makes us stressed. Have a system that you trust. And I suggest a system that's outside of email. Email is not brilliantly designed for being a task manager. Use lists. I'm obsessed by lists. In fact, I am incredibly sad and nerdy when it comes to lists, but they work incredibly well. Personally I use a system called Getting Things Done, which is a system created by a guy called David Allen. But there are lots of other systems out there. The key is to create good lists.

Finally we turn our attention to delegating. I'm a huge fan of delegating. Why do something yourself when you can get someone else to do it is my attitude. Maybe that's a bit extreme, but there are a lot of situations where we can delegate out the work that we're doing. What you need to do is establish what the right criteria are. I would suggest that you need to be spending your time doing what you're good at. If you're not good at something, get someone else who is good at it to do it instead. They'll do it a lot quicker, and you can charge out the time you would have spent doing that on things that you actually enjoy. And that's the second thing, do what you enjoy. What's the point of being your own boss if you're going to spend loads of time doing jobs you absolutely hate? It makes no sense. What you need to be asking yourself is where is your time most profitably spent? And you need to compare that to what you're actually doing. If you find that there are jobs that you're doing that are not the most profitable, not the most enjoyable, then delegate them. Great examples of that are bookkeeping, office admin, arranging meetings, invoicing. All this kind of stuff you really shouldn't be doing. The truth is that if you get yourself organized, if you delegate stuff, if you remove distractions, you're going to get so much more done, and you will end up working less hours, making more money, and be a lot happier at the end of it.

Conclusion

Conclusion

So there you go; you now know everything you need to, to run a successful web design business. Hopefully, you've learned that being a freelance web designer is about a lot more than just coding and designing. It's about great marketing, having a solid sales process, offering amazing customer support and getting organized. We need to build a lifestyle business a business where we can work less, earn more, work on projects that we love and work to live, rather than living to work.

Made in the USA
Columbia, SC
16 May 2019